C000099109

At the Crossroads

poems by

Lina Belar

Finishing Line Press
Georgetown, Kentucky

At the Crossroads

ACKNOWLEDGMENTS

How a Century Farm Begins—Talking Stick
Tumbleweed—Talking Stick
Watching the Anhinga Bird in Sarasota—Talking Stick
The Future of the World—Talking Stick
The White Ibis—1st Place Award Brainerd Writers Alliance
Recognition—Citation LOMP Helen Pappas Memorial Award

Publisher: Leah Huete de Maines
Editor: Christen Kincaid
Cover Art: Lina Belar
Authors Photo: Jean-Louis Monfraix
Cover Design: Elizabeth Maines McCleavy

Order online: www.finishinglinepress.com
also available on amazon.com

Author inquiries and mail orders:
Finishing Line Press
PO Box 1626
Georgetown, Kentucky 40324
USA

Contents

Dedicated to Cynthia D. Belar

City Sidewalks

In the boulevard between the curved walk
peopled by runners and bicyclists
parading in neon colored spandex,
and the four-lane highway where traffic
rages in obedience to precision controlled
traffic lights, lies a springy turf of grass,
home to a world of miniature flowers.
No signs draw attention to their existence
but I am of an age where a morning walk
is more a quiet saunter and, like children and dogs,
I am easily distracted. Today, it's not shiny toys
or gum wrappers that catch my eye but the tiny,
unnamed, unheralded harbingers of spring.

I notice first the wild strawberries,
Their daisy-like flowers towering
two inches above the rest. By summer,
they might produce fruit for the birds
if the lawn-mower spares them. Closer to ground,
blue flax flowers rise carefully above
swords of grass, stars dotting the heavens
above a miniature world. Nestled at the soil line
are pea-sized yellow flowers, like the wooden balls
of a miniature croquet game, abandoned
when the players stopped for tea.
I imagine joining the game, treading carefully
around the sharp blades of grass while high above
a fluffy dandelion explodes, showering me with silk.

Nameless

The waiter did not know the name of the flowers
that clung to the restaurant wall as though a child
had crumpled red tissue paper and tucked it
among the leaves of a vine.

But he pointed out to me the poinsettias
topped with leaves like red and white sabers
guarding their secret flowers. He noticed them daily
and he liked them, but he didn't know their names either.

All around us are unknown flowers, no less beautiful
for lack of nomenclature. Perhaps flowers, like people,
could wear little tags so that they could be greeted
warmly by name, even the weeds.

Under the Apple Tree

When I was a child, I could sit
under the apple tree, my back
against the trunk, and watch
as a shimmering veil descended
from the tips of its branches
until the whole space beneath the tree
was enveloped in a cone of golden silence.
Inside this space, no sound intruded,
not the traffic from the nearby street
nor the tuneful singing of my mother
as she raked the new cut grass.
There were leaves on that apple tree,
and blossoms. And perhaps
the comforting hum I heard was bees
but at the time I was sure it was angels.

Summer Nights

There were nights on the boat
when we listened to the weather
on the short wave radio

then went up on deck where
my sister and I lay on our
backs and counted the stars.

"Will it rain?" says our mother
meaning—will we be stuck
down below in the cramped cabin

playing cards and eating Oreos
while the Tecumseh engine burns
oil and drowns out other sounds.

"There should be a good breeze by noon,"
our father answers meaning—we will
skate the surface of the waves,

sails raised fore and aft,
my sister and I on the foredeck,
backs to the cabin, faces to the wind.

Our father always knew
what the weather would be.
Night after night he disagreed

with the weatherman,
most times he was right.
I don't know why he listened.

Those nights we spent anchored
in the harbor, the lights of cities
far away, the Milky Way a trail

of powdered sugar dividing the sky,
our mother taught us the patterns
of the stars, their names and stories.

Cassiopia, her queenly chair, Orion,
his dagger studded with jewels,
the seven sisters of the Pleiades.

In time, we'd go below to sleep in bunks
nestled in the bow of the boat.
"Tell me a story," my sister would say.

I would tell her about gentle queen Marie
who lived beneath the sea and spent her days
weaving lace from seaweed and pearls.

As I drifted off to sleep, I listened to the water
lap the side of the hull and felt the gentle slap
of the ropes against the mast.

Despite the warnings of the weatherman
tomorrow would be a nice day.
Our father had said so.

Strawberry Moon

Last night
the strawberry moon
rose pinkly
over the gunmetal lake
casting a trail of silver shards.
Each step a hazard
for the mermaid's
fragile feet.

Welcome Mat

In late fall, birds with black taffeta wings
peck at branches in the dying birch,
drill holes in its brittle bark
looking for burrowing insects.

Beneath the tree's aging skin
hides a borer, clueless that his work
has left a trail of golden sawdust
glued like a welcome mat outside his door.

How A Century Farm Begins

Inside a small farmhouse where
women grind grain for the bread
while the wind blows, and the men
wrest a living from the rock-laden soil,
through hot summers and bitter cold winters,
the grain, seed for next year's planting,
lies protected from heat and cold and wet
in a tightly sealed room with no windows
in the middle of the house.

Children are forbidden to play here.
Mice and rodents dare not chance the wrath
of the farmer's wife with her sharp blade,
Like fairy tale princesses the seeds slumber
in safety, dreaming of languid summer days,
blue skies and occasional rain.

In spring, the door to the room is opened
all but a small amount of the seed removed.
The fields are sown, produce grain
to feed the livestock, cows give birth,
provide milk for their young with enough left over
for the human babies who will soon grow
large enough to help plant the seed,
cut the grain, thrash it and store it
for the next generation, in the room
with no windows in the middle of the house.

Crossroads

Driving the back roads
of west central Minnesota
it's impossible not to notice
how many signs point to Wolf Lake.

The town itself is small,
with a newly remodeled gas station,
an active VFW club,
several abandoned buildings.

The Kinnunen general store
is closed and shuttered,
its second and last letters
missing for decades.

At the crossroads, signs
point to other distant towns.
All roads lead to Wolf Lake,
All roads leave here, too.

Tumbleweed

This morning as the dawn appeared
I saw a three-foot tumbleweed,
its thinnest branches covered
with a rime of morning frost
lodged between the markers in my garden

It must have blown here in the night
bouncing all the way from North Dakota
spinning and turning on the wind
trailing winter in its wake and I
could only imagine what that was like.

Did it tumble its way along the arrowed
highways, avoiding passenger cars
and eighteen wheelers, or did it stick to the fields
tuck in its many legs and roll across the empty plains
until it skittered across the river into Minnesota?

Like an exhausted messenger, sent to warn the king,
the tumbleweed just sat there in my frozen garden,
speechless, shivering at each gust of northern wind.
As sun melted morning frost, its limbs it began to sparkle.
Only then did it tell me why it had come.

Street Repair

All month, the big yellow machines go back and forth
on the road by my house, holes are dug,
artifacts, both mysterious and commonplace,
are laid within the bowels of the earth.

Cement trucks pour ribbons of curb and gutter,
driveways and sidewalks are smoothed,
neat bright lines to complement the green lawns
until only the dirt road remains.

Today they are working on that.
One truck spews a narrow line of brown dirt
from beneath its belly. Another blades the windrow
into a carefully measured depth.

A tank truck travels up and down the road
water spraying from its hind end, followed by
a big red tractor pulling a wagon-like contraption
filled with scrap iron, tires and rubble.

Its sixteen fat tires smooth and compact the road.
At noon, a white truck with discreet lettering
pulls up and parks across the street.
A man in a neon green shirt hops out.

He walks to the middle of the road,
puts a shovel in the now smooth surface
and places a few scoops of dirt in a plastic bag.
The small pile that remains seems a desecration.

History Lesson

In Lake Bled, a thousand year old church stands on its own island.
Ten centuries ago, says the tour guide, pilgrims stopped here on their way
to the Holy Land, ascending the steps to the chapel on their knees.

What were they praying for? Safe journey? Forgiveness of sins?
What drove them to travel thousands of miles to a place they'd never been,
perhaps to bring home a piece of saint's bone as memento?

Today, we row across the lake in handmade wooden boats,
pay a few coins to ring the bell in the steeple, purchase photographs
of the church as souvenirs of the peace that now blesses Slovenia.

Surrounding the lake are the foothills of the southern Alps. A short drive
brings us to Bled Castle, where a miniature city fortified for defense
by moat and drawbridge reminds us that life was not always so peaceful.

Ten centuries ago, we're told, danger traveled these valleys. First the Huns,
looking for young blondes they could breed, then soldiers of the Ottoman
    Empire,
taking young boys for their armies, girls for their harems.

Napoleon marched his armies through here on his way to Russia.
For the peasants who lived in the valleys, flight
was their only defense, the castle their only refuge.

We pile back into our cars and drive a few miles to Vintgar Gorge
where the River Sava has cut a natural canyon through the limestone valley
before emptying its green glacial waters into the Mediterranean.

Some trees have died here lately, uprooted by a spring storm. Forty feet tall,
they hang headfirst down the side of the gorge. During the war some
men died here, tumbling the slopes to the river until the green waters ran red.

The Silence of Slovenia

In the silence of Slovenia
women sing an ancient song
as they row their wooden boats
across the lake.

Po jezero, po jezero
a tune my father still recalled
after nearly eighty years
in foreign lands.

In the silence of Slovenia
church bells ring from dawn to dusk
like the ones that called to me
at seventeen.

Ave, Ave Verum corpus,
natum de Maria Virgine,
the faith of centuries
coursing through my veins.

In the silence of Slovenia
the weight of history presses hard
on each square foot of land
where armies fought.

But now in gentle valleys
flowers bloom where once was blood
and soldiers' sons paint
shutters every year.

** Latin Hymn that has been set to music by various composers
including Wolfgang Amadeus Mozart (Ave Verum Corpus) It dates
from the 14th century. Hail, Hail True Body, born of the Virgin Mary*

The Bells of Slovenia

During World War One, the bronze bells that hung
in every church in every town and valley
were melted down to make weapons for the Great War.

Imagine how astonished those bells must have been.
Instead of peals of joy glorifying all creation
they were to become instruments of destruction.

Not surprisingly, the spirit of each bell departed,
flew up to the heavens to join other celestial spirits
where they waited, warmed by starlight and protected by infinity.

Later, when war was over, the iron factory at Jesenice
began making bells of steel to replace
those taken from the churches during the war.

Chapel bells, cathedral bells, small bells, large bells,
even one weighing six tons. They made more than 2000 bells,
enough to replace all the bells in every church Slovenia.

When the spirits learned of this they rejoiced.
Back to earth they swarmed like meteorites
re-entering the atmosphere to add their warmth to the cold steel.

*Jesenice is a Slovenian town near the Austrian border notable for mining
and iron making industries.*

Recognition

At the entrance to the market in Ljubljana an old woman
has settled herself on the pavement, a black and white kitten
on her lap, aluminum cane by her side.

She holds a stringed instrument made of wood. There are spaces
for eight strings but only one is attached. The woman saws at it
with a curved bow, making a small discordant sound.

The belly of the instrument is papered with pictures,
Blessed Virgin Mary, St. Joseph, the Pope, and the head shot
of a young girl, perhaps her daughter, with the heavy-lidded eyes

and prominent nose that I had when I was twelve.
Instead of walking past the old woman, I stop and drop some coins
in the box by her side, hold up my camera, make hand gestures

asking her permission for a photograph. As I snap the picture she smiles,
perhaps in recognition of my familiar features or the shared
realization that now I know how I will look, when I am an old woman.

Sarasota Bay

This bay has something for everyone.
Fish for the pelicans, the ducks and the gulls
the herons who wait at the shoreline.
Fishing boats, crab boats, leaving each dawn

with a clatter of nets and lazy black smoke
that lays on the water when the diesels cough
their first good breath of the morning.
Motor boats and sailboats, little novice sailors

who flutter like butterflies in the light afternoon breeze
while their instructor shouts lessons through a bullhorn.
The kayaks, the paddleboards, the jet boat with its airplane engine
drawing hostile looks from tourists perched on their verandas.

A photographer captures an osprey
as it snatches a fish from the water,
another poses a wedding couple
on the broken pilings of the old fishing pier.

Cruise ships, dining rooms that move
from pier to pier, getting fatter each year.
Old men and young children fishing
under the bridge at sunset.

And dolphins, especially the dolphins,
turning graceful cartwheels in the water
surfacing now and again, the visible crescent
of a great submerged paddlewheel.

Evening Cruise

Along the waterfront, cruise ships
with polished chrome and spotless hulls
wait for evening passengers
to shuffle up the ramp.

Some, a little tipsy already,
but happy to be here
to be wined and dined
while an invisible loudspeaker

claiming to be the captain
tells them what a good time
they are going to have.
On every piling a pelican
looks on, head tucked into his neck.

Storm over Sarasota Bay

This morning, the fog smoothed the bay's surface
until it gleamed like dull aluminum.
Later, the wind shifted to the north,
back-combing the palm trees.

Now waves pound the shoreline
drowning all other sounds.
I watch as two kayaks skim toward shore,
yellow bodied insects with flashing limbs.

Sturdy fishing boats return to safe harbor,
cheated again of a good day's catch.
Even the pelicans are forced to beat
a wing or two to stay aloft.

I like the sound of the sea at work,
hammering the sand, working up a sweat.
It's tough on shorebirds who on gentler days
pick delicately at water's edge
in search of tasty morsels.

By noon, the sea has turned a killer green.
A cowboy in a speedboat
heads toward open water
tossing waves aside like feathers.

All day the sea churns, each sharply pointed wave
spits white foam as it gives another tug
at the bottom, turning the water brown.
Breakers crest higher and further from the beach.

Now and then, there's a brief breathing space.
no bigger than a comma. A pelican
skims close to the waves, lands in the trough
between jagged peaks. Perhaps something good
will be stirred up by all this activity.

By late afternoon the sky has changed.
patches of blue appear, clouds lighten,
but the sea is still mad. It throbs and squirms
as though there are monsters to restrain.

Water roils and boils as old insults are recalled.
Toxic oil spills. Atomic bomb tests.
When I was a child they used to explode
old bombs on the Chesapeake Bay.

A day later, fish would float belly-up
on the outgoing tide, lifeless eyes
turned up to heaven. All the seas are connected.
Each remembers the pain done to another.

Watching the Anhinga Bird in Sarasota

For two hours every day that I am here
the anhinga perches on the seawall above the bay
turning this way and that
until he's found the perfect angle of sun.
He swivels his long neck to check
that no one is watching.
What is this? He's vain?
Neck of a snake,
body gone south like a pear.
He unfolds wings like a bat.
Beneath his dull dark wrapper
lurk white feathers like ivory
stolen from Africa,
hidden from poachers,
he shows these treasures
to no one
but the sea.

The White Ibis

As soon as I leave the pool
the White Ibis returns, hops
to the top of the aluminum ladder
stands poised on one orange leg
looks down his curved orange beak at the world.
Satisfied all is well, he picks his way
along the inner rim of the pool
sipping chlorinated water like champagne.
When no one is looking he lights a long cigarillo,
blows smoke circles at the sun.

The Future of the World

I am waiting for the day you can't buy pens anymore.
Who needs a writing instrument once telepathy replaces speech?
Already, most communication has been reduced to the fingertip.

With one swipe you can sign your name, message a friend,
capture a picture. Pens and pencils are but crutches
for those unable to see how evolution is at work.

The tap follows the thought and soon the tips of our fingers
will become the conduit for all that is glorious and beautiful
in our minds as well as the sad and forlorn.

From final tap to telepathy we will once again be able to hear
the vast symphony of the earth as it goes about its business
of living and eating and dying.

As I write this, I am watching a great blue heron poised
at water's edge, waves breaking across his bony feet
waiting for the sea to bring him his breakfast.

Not Alone

The traffic on the nearby bridge
thrums with the sound of trucks and motorcycles.
It's a sound that says you're not alone,
but the sound I want to hear
is the sound of the surf,
the one that never lies.
The one that says you are alone and yet,
are we not also part of you?
The water and minerals that float in your veins
are also found in the creatures of the sea,
even the scallop who likes his cadmium.
Even the rare ones like you.

Milton Keynes UK
Ingram Content Group UK Ltd.
UKHW010701090524
442467UK00003B/99